THE PERSPECTIVE

A Shift to Life's Realizations

WYATT BROOKS

BALBOA.
PRESS

A DIVISION OF HAY HOUSE

Balboa Press books may be ordered through booksellers or by contacting:

Balboa Press
A Division of Hay House
1663 Liberty Drive
Bloomington, IN 47403
www.balboapress.com
1 (877) 407-4847

Because of the dynamic nature of the Internet, any web addresses or
links contained in this book may have changed since publication and
may no longer be valid. The views expressed in this work are solely those
of the author and do not necessarily reflect the views of the publisher,
and the publisher hereby disclaims any responsibility for them.

The author of this book does not dispense medical advice or prescribe the use
of any technique as a form of treatment for physical, emotional, or medical
problems without the advice of a physician, either directly or indirectly. The
intent of the author is only to offer information of a general nature to help
you in your quest for emotional and spiritual well-being. In the event you use
any of the information in this book for yourself, which is your constitutional
right, the author and the publisher assume no responsibility for your actions.

Any people depicted in stock imagery provided by Thinkstock are
models, and such images are being used for illustrative purposes only.
Certain stock imagery © Thinkstock.

Print information available on the last page.

ISBN: 978-1-5043-4917-8 (sc)
ISBN: 978-1-5043-4919-2 (hc)
ISBN: 978-1-5043-4918-5 (e)

Library of Congress Control Number: 2016900970

Balboa Press rev. date: 02/23/2016

CONTENTS

To those seeking to follow not,

but to create by the stroke of their own brush.

CHAPTER 1

THE CONTRAST

I was given the gift of not being born into a family with much financial prosperity. There is a sense of gratitude and appreciation acquired in growing up knowing the value of a dollar, in being raised in a nine-hundred-square-foot home, and, most importantly, in indulging in comforting meals made with what's left in the pantry. Despite my family's prior financial stance, my mother and father made every effort possible to provide for my sister and me, ensuring that we would be given a life with many more opportunities to strive and succeed than they were given at our age. One of the many ways in which my parents made these efforts was in providing my sister and me with a private-school education.

From preschool through the eighth grade, I attended a school in an impecunious suburb on the Southern California grid. Though the establishment was very limited on funds and teaching and recreational equipment, it served as a very valuable lesson-provider in my life. Unfortunately, I cannot recall any significant information I had retained in the classrooms at my elementary school that had derived from textbooks or focused lectures, apart from the essential alphabet lessons and algebraic equations. However, the lessons I learned and have taken from my many years at this school were of those experienced outside the classroom.

We all face widespread discrimination and directed prejudice at various points in our lives, and I was fortunate enough to experience such encounters at an early age. Quite contrary to what we normally see in our world today, I was often discriminated against for my fairness in color because I was seen as a minority in an environment that was primarily attended by darker skinned Hispanics. Along with the racial and the superficial prejudices, many of my peers—myself included—were often discriminated against for the amount of money our parents made - something that should not hold much importance in the personal life of a child and his societal relationships.

One would not think that there would be any sort of financial discrimination in an impoverished educational setting amongst lower income students, but the crass truth stood that if you had but a dollar less than the student beside you, you were immediately viewed as a lesser.

I took the discomfort and uneasiness of this particular section of my childhood to motivate me in believing in something greater; believing in something, someplace, where I could grow as an individual without the restraints of such a hindering, and sometimes toxic environment.

As I neared the seventh grade, it was time to start considering where I was to attend high school. I had relative attending a rather prestigious school in an outlying, affluent community not more than a half hour's drive from where I had lived at the time. I immediately took interest in the school. I saw an opportunity to experience what I had been yearning for, and what I had known I was not only capable of accomplishing but also deserving. It would be an environment where I would be provided with an opportunity to excel academically without the restraints and lack of resources of my elementary school. I inquired as much about the school as I could and often visited, which enabled me to visualize attending the establishment in my near future. My goal was viewed as far-fetched and out of reach by many who were anything but encouraging. I, however, persevered in catapulting myself toward the academic environment I knew I was deserving and worthy of experiencing.

Through years of academic diligence, I found myself sitting in the front of the classroom at the high school where I had aspired to be—my very real, very tangible manifestation of what was once seen as a far-fetched dream. The shift of environment did not stop in the shiny new campus and the state-of-the-art technology found in the classrooms but continued in the energy I recognized in the students and faculty themselves. I immediately found myself in a place of encouragement and of helping others succeed. I do not remember experiencing any sort of competition or "survival of the fittest" notions in my new location but a sheltered and loving place where I felt I could be myself and be loved for it, and where succeeding in whatever I put my mind to was always encouraged.

My alma mater was a college-preparatory school, and it was not considered unusual for a fourteen-year-old freshman to have where he or she would attend university accurately figured out. I remember walking into my academic counselor's office one morning to discuss my class schedule when a poster advertising a university in London caught my attention. I had family who lived abroad and the idea of being an addition to the list of relatives who had either made their excursions across the pond or had originated there had always been very appealing to me. From that moment on, I held this particular university as my utmost priority and next goal to bring forth into manifestation.

I often held the image of living in London in my mind and kept replaying the mental motion of walking through the city streets as award-winning films and novels made them out to be. I felt excited yet calm every time I gave this goal attention; I knew it would happen, and I knew I would be as happy when it happened as I was when I was mentally and emotionally preparing for it.

When it came time to formally discuss with academic counselors and teachers about university in my later years, I was often called a "dreamer" and specifically remember being laughed at as if my goal was again seen as unreachable or senseless. I remained focused on the end result, again believing in something greater, and soon thereafter found myself seated onboard a British Airways Boeing 777 en route to London. I had a scholarship to the very university in London that I had envisioned attending years before.

Upon arriving in the United Kingdom, I was overwhelmed with heightened joy and gratitude. London was pleasingly everything I had imagined it to be and so much more. Coming from a very relaxed Southern California environment and inherited lifestyle, the grandiosity and business of the city were satisfyingly refreshing. There was always something to do, the sense of fashion was outstanding, and the magnitude of British accents was very entertaining. The overall lifestyle of Londoners is one I would recommend to be experienced by everyone.

After a week of sightseeing and adventuring around the city, it was finally time to transition from my hotel room to my dorm at university. I was immediately overjoyed with the historic campus and the diversity of the students. Attending a university in arguably the world's most culturally diverse city meant making friendships with people from near and wide. Finally being able to experience this reality in the flesh, after so many years of dreaming and anticipating, sometimes brought tears to my eyes in bliss of seeing it finally manifested.

University life in London was very different from what I had expected it to be, based on what it was made out to be in the States. There were very many circumstances that called for a sudden sense of independence and self-care that I had not yet been introduced to in my sheltered lifestyle back home. How and with whom I decided to spend the twenty-four hours of my day was entirely up to me, and the consequences of my sometimes spontaneous decisions were also dealt with completely on my own.

In the midst of all the excitement of my new move came an unannounced and life-changing encounter. I was in the university's cafeteria serving myself lunch when I was greeted with by an overly forward man whom I had not seen before. He was older in age but seemed to have a very energetic demeanor. "Hello, gorgeous," he said. Astounded, I nervously greeted him with a simple hello and carried on my way.

I did not recall seeing him on campus until days later when I overheard him greeting yet another student and addressing her too by "gorgeous." I had immediately dismissed all discomforting feelings towards the mysterious man and understood him to be a charming person who perhaps attempted to be familiar with the students in his own way. I was also new to the country and unfamiliar with British mannerisms, leading me to decide to not think too heavily on our encounter.

Sometime after, I was again serving myself in the cafeteria when this man—whom I later found to be an administrator at my university—approached me and stated that he would be joining my friends and me for dinner that evening. I welcomed the administrator to join us, and introduced him to my friends who were already seated at the table.

During dinner, conversation began on a pleasant note and everything seemed exceptionally ordinary, though as the night progressed, the administrator began to give the impression that he had some sort of psychic abilities. He continued to address each individual around the table and shared progressively personal information about him or her aloud. It was my turn. He began to state what I considered the painfully obvious facts that anyone I walked past along High Street could gather. However, he later gave false accusations of me, including those related to my sexuality and how I expressed it. I found his words painful and unbearable, leaving me with nothing other than the need to excuse myself from the table for the evening. Thoughts swarmed my head, attempting to comprehend what I had just experienced and why it had been necessary.

On my way back up to my room that evening, I was approached by two university resident assistants who had overheard the administrator's conversation at my table. The RAs insisted that I kept my distance from the man as they personally did not trust him. They continued in sharing that he routinely pulled this "psychic" stunt to all vulnerable incoming freshmen each year.

Every time I encountered the administrator thereafter, he approached and addressed me with more suggestive comments and accusations. Not only were his words discomforting and hurtful to hear, but they also caused much embarrassment as they were made in front of other students on campus. However, I was so caught up with trying to settle into my new home that I did my best in dismissing his efforts to bother me and never felt as though I should have reported his inappropriate behavior.

Months went by and it was now October. I was serving myself dinner in the cafeteria when I had felt someone grab my shoulders from behind me, and shove his knee up my rear. Turning around and seeing the same face I had expected it to be left me feeling incredibly violated, disgusted, and seemingly submissive to the degree in which he was now abusing his power towards me. I firmly announced that his actions were far from acceptable and watched him walk away laughing. I returned to my friends, sharing what had just happened. Everyone quickly began to share the same feelings of disgust that were running through me. As we were discussing the severity of the issue, the administrator approached our table and warned me "Just be thankful that that was my knee." I excused myself from the table, climbed up the staircase to the third floor, entered my room and made the long-distance phone call to my parents in California to inform them of my situation and to ask them for their advice. I had spoke with my Father and remember hearing the hurt in his voice when I gave him the news. I was advised to call the London police to report the administrator's unacceptable behavior. Nearly an hour later, two police officers arrived on campus and took my statement and that of a witness. The administrator was arrested on campus the next morning.

The events following the assault can be understood as anything but comforting. I was 5,000 miles away from home and taking matters day by day on my own. My stress load left such a negative impact on me that I was diagnosed depressed and prescribed medication to alleviate my condition and accompanying anxiety. I had such a distaste for life that I began to partake in harmful and disrespectful behavior—I had lost my flame that once burned so bright.

London's vibrant city life had been washed and greyed; nothing seemed meaningful and nothing brought much happiness into my experience. On two occasions, I found my body sprawled across my bedroom floor coming back into consciousness after overdosing on my medication. I remember clearly being hooked up to a heart monitor at a nearby hospital and hearing the alarm ignite because my heart rate was severely low. I think the only thing that brought my heart rate back up was the fear of death when it was staring me right in the face. Why any of us turn to self harm during circumstances of distress can only justly be understood by the individual and his or her own take on the events leading to such behavior. I saw myself as a failure, and could not imagine what my circumstances would have been like if I would have listened to the discouragers and had not gone to London to begin with. I took complete blame for my assault and felt as though I had wasted countless days on striving to get to a place where I would only then suffer. I could no longer cope with the lost time and finances, and I wanted to escape—even if only for a little while.

Naturally, attending classes was not on the path towards my healing. Thankfully, my university understood the matter and suggested that I withdraw from my Fall semester courses, ensuring that I would still be able to reside on campus without having to return back home to the United States as I had already paid for my housing and tuition in full prior to the beginning of the school year. Though it was extremely helpful that my university had allowed me to stay, I was then faced with the predicament of being on my own all throughout the day with nothing to occupy myself with. Not having a sense of direction during the day was extremely detrimental as it only made matters worse in that it allowed the depression to occupy my mind, preventing and prohibiting me from recovery.

I remember the days being exceptionally dark. No matter where I was or what I was doing, the painful memories of humiliation and ridicule accompanied with incisive feelings of neglect from other students soiled any beaconing rays of hope for change and a new beginning. Because I had felt the only way in which my life could unfold was backwards, I decided to return back to California for a short while as I waited for the storm that was my first semester to pass.

Upon my arrival back into the United States, I at least felt a sense of familiarity and safeness. I had returned home in early November with anticipation of staying through until at least the Thanksgiving Holiday. Being in proximity of my beloved friends and family provided such needed emotional lifts and the ability to finally smile again. However, because I had so suddenly hopped on a plane halfway across the world, I had not taken precautionary measures in ensuring I had everything I needed before I embarked. It was only a matter of days after my arrival when I had completely run out of my antidepressant and tranquilizing medications prescribed to me in the United Kingdom. Though I was on such a heightened emotional vibration in being with my family, my body quickly presented signs of withdrawal from the medication. Quitting anything cold turkey can introduce severe consequences on the body I soon found.

I immediately fell ill and was no longer in a position to cherish my time with my family and friends as I had hoped. Because I had been prescribed my medication in a different country, I had to continue my dosage in that same country and could not seek similar prescriptions from my physician in the United States. Being able to see my beloved family and friends again gave me the strength I needed to return to London and terminate any lasting complications that prohibited me from completely enjoying something I had worked so hard for. My mother's last words to me at the departure gate, "Kick ass, son."

Upon my arrival back into the United Kingdom, I had reached the decision of withdrawing from the university altogether, but refrained from doing so until I was reimbursed my paid tuition in light of events that took place. The Holiday season was fast approaching and the university was not showing any sign of giving me an answer in what was then the near future. Since I had only come back from California, I was not in the financial position to return again. I instead spent Christmas with my grandmother in the Swiss Alps. My grandmother was currently moving from one apartment to another, giving me the opportunity to provide my help and to take my mind off of my life in London for a while. Being situated in such a prestigious part of the world provided much deserved tranquility. The Christmas of 2013 was one of heavy lifting and of countless trips to the local recycling and waste center, but the Christmas of 2013 was a happy one.

The Holiday cheer was short lived and it was time to return to London. It was a new year, and I had hoped to start afresh at university and focus on bettering my life and shifting my future in a more positive direction. However, after returning to campus I soon found that the cold stares and isolation from my peers and friends washed away any hope for change. As word of the assault spread throughout the campus, students began to keep their distance.

I ate my meals alone, stayed in my room, and felt the depression flowing throughout my body once again. Hello, old friend.

I received news from the finance department that I was not to be reimbursed my paid tuition because I had passed the withdrawal deadline. I felt so utterly aggravated that the university was using technicalities with such a delicate situation. I had no other choice but to wash my hands and return home for good. It took weeks of contemplation, but I felt in my heart that I could no longer tolerate the hurt of staying in London when everything around me seemed to have already fallen apart.

Packing my bags had been the most difficult situation I had gone through in London as the feelings running throughout my body were completely opposite to those when I was departing Southern California just the summer before. It was on March 7th, 2014 when I saw the aerial view of my beloved dream fade into the distance from the Boeing 777 window.

Returning home was anything but easy. Returning meant total defeat, effortlessly succumbing to the brutalities of my past experiences in London. I was in an utmost delicate stage, one of complete lack of faith and of lost hope. I had no direction, no aspiring goals to achieve, and saw no light at the end of the tunnel. Though the painful truth of waking up back in California after such a long internal and external battle felt so unsatisfying, the most excruciating realization was that of seeing my beloved family again and being so emotionally numb that I could not bring myself to be uplifted in their presence.

From the moment of my return to the moment when I could truthfully say that I had finally gained enough strength to again stand on my own two feet again, 7 months had passed. From that of the actual incident, one whole year. During those 7 months, I had gone through a very crucial part of my life that I identify as being my Shift of Perspective. In this personal shift, I have come to many realizations of truths of life, I have strengthened myself internally and become in tune with my higher frequency, gained awe-inspiring outlooks on a widespread range of topics, and achieved the ultimate success I imagined possible. I am in complete awareness that I have been enlightened and inspired to turn unto the world in complete faith that what I have gained through my shift is to be shared. I do not seek to impress anyone with my successes and triumphs, but rather to impress upon everyone that they too can achieve their own individual enlightenment in their own individual lives in igniting the awareness of true power to create worlds held within.

CHAPTER 2

INTRODUCTION OF SOURCE

For as long as I can remember I have struggled with adhering to traditions and succumbing to the "what is" so many people build their day-to-day lives on. As formerly expressed in the introduction of my personal life contrast, I had received private, Catholic education from early childhood until my early adulthood at high school. As I began to identify and transition into the individual that I am today, I repeatedly found myself questioning the systems our society place so importantly—primarily that of religion and how tradition and rules served as the apparent structural foundation supporting these greater organized belief systems. I can quite clearly remember having always approached religion with a great sense of uncertainty and intimidation, feeling uneasiness towards acting out in a way that had been so unnatural to me and never quite reaching the feeling the wholesomeness of God's adoration to the degree in which I knew I could.

Expanding my focus from that which I was so directly affected and challenging myself to think about how not only Catholicism was structured, but how most, if not all, other religions came into fruition as the massive factions within a greater community that they are today, it was finally evident why the religion I had grown up practicing did not sit so well within me. After much contemplation, I found that in more instances than not, religions are based upon one or a select group of individuals' experiences with God. Later, these personal experiences were documented and handed down to another select few to set guidelines, boundaries and traditions, exemplifying how every individual thereafter should act out and contribute to the community in order to be accepted and labeled as a man of goodness and judged positively on his final day.

I immediately felt discord between all that had been taught to me throughout the years, however, I had never felt more clarity than I had when coming to this realization. I later partook in more internal practices to set out a new perspective of God, and so eagerly sought how I was to lead my life with a personal, spiritual experience with God as my main objective and only focus.

I still very much adored God and finally began to feel the utmost adoration reciprocated onto me that I had so yearned for in my years of growing and individualizing into my adulthood, yet in a completely new and refreshing perspective that provided internal peace and easiness. I continued my quest to strengthen my personal experience with God and soon found that there was a number of spiritual and motivational expressers worldwide that had disconnected themselves from these greater monopoly religions to find their own personal experiences with God. In sifting and sorting through these "awakening" teachings I found through my research, I addressed which perspectives felt most achievable, and did my absolute best in beginning the practice of applying and fusing these new perspectives into my day-to-day life.

Naturally, identifying the very root of all that is and all that ever will be was a great place to start in the path towards my personal experience with God. I immediately paired like with like in my research and found that there was no difference in face value between the scientific teachings and description of energy from the spiritual teachings and concepts of God. In other words, I found that by definition, God and energy are both expressed similarly. Throughout my childhood, I never understood the lasting argument between truths of spirituality and of science. I was presented with an immediate sense of satisfaction in coming to understand that what I believed to be the core of both focus points had in fact been similar.

I was in search of a term or an identifying title that would allow myself to link both the scientific and spiritual ideas, which I believed wholeheartedly indeed did coexist. In analyzing and dissecting the matter further, I became rather literal and saw the two at face value. I believed God to be the source of all that is and all that will ever be. God is everlasting, indefinable, infinite energy that not only brought forth everything into physical being, but is of everything in our life experience. Of course! God is source of all that is and all that ever will be; God is source. And with ease, I was finally able to identify God with not so much a title with underlying feelings of uncertainty and intimidation expressed by religious leaders and teachers in my life, but rather a lucid, mental and emotional grasp of God. Again, a sense of clarity flowed through, and I was immediately inspired to act and challenge myself further to understand how my relationship with Source of all that is would follow, and how I would use my relationship with Source to positively impact the world.

CHAPTER 3

EXPERIENCING SOURCE

Finally bringing myself to the ability of identifying Source, I was in a position of allowing myself the continuation of the spiritual and healing journey I began in returning to California. With the new perspective of Source I had allowed myself, I was given a clean slate, or a sturdy foundation in which I could rebuild my life. I had gone through an unexplainable rush of freedom and abundance in ridding all negative beliefs and misconceptions associated with Source. I no longer feared being watched over; I had finally disburdened myself of old connotations that are otherwise linked with Source.

Being able to identify Source as "Source", I was immediately provided with my very own untouched idea of what Source is, without the intimidating stigmas that are usually associated with Source. As with all things, one cannot possibly offer split energy between two ideas, emotions, or things in our physical or vibrational experiences and expect to receive in full one over the other. Of Source, there is only utmost love and adoration, acceptance and wholesomeness. Of Source, there is no judgment or cruelty, no pain or absence. I also speak confidently in saying that there is no such existence of evil, there is only discord, or misalignment with Source. It is evident to me now that when we are feeling incomplete, depressed, angry, and all of the other magnitude of names society has given titles to poor-emotions, we are merely out of range of Source and the adoration of Source energy implemented in everything around us. With this, it is understood that there is much importance in being tuned in to our emotions and the way we are feeling. I know all too well that at first glance this comes off to be quite the chore, but I can assure that giving attention to the way we are feeling plays the lead role in receiving all that we are wanting.

One shared belief concerning Source amongst most, if not all, religions and practices is that Source is all that is and all that ever shall be. Digging deeper, it is understood that we as human beings are of this greater multiplication of creations that Source is and expresses itself as. Literally speaking, we too are of Source and hold Source energy within our bodies, providing us with the possibility to create our own realities and circumstances. We as human beings—capsules of Source energy—

hold the power to create our own realities and

experiences through virtue of the thoughts and

feelings we vibrate. We hold the power within

to create.

CHAPTER 4

INTRODUCTION TO LOA

Some four to five years ago, I was introduced to a valuable piece of knowledge that I have only since started to understand further. At any given moment, we encounter what we call universal laws. Quite simply, these laws are directives that we all follow knowingly or otherwise. There is one universal law, however, that I hold most important in my life and have come to finally understand more clearly through my spiritual practices and further understanding of Source—the Law of Attraction.

In completely grasping that which is the Law of Attraction, it is easiest to begin with the very breakdown of what exactly is at play—like attracts like. We often hear of karma, and are frequently reminded that what goes around, comes around, but most often do not understand to which extent these ideologies are true and can be knowingly applied and incorporated into our daily lives.

Now that Source is more easily understood as the immeasurable energy held at the very core of all creation, we understand that we too hold within Source energy. This concept took some time for me to completely grasp as I felt most guilty for comparing myself with Source. It was not until I dug to the root of the underlying truth that I was finally able to make peace with what was at hand. We remember that God, Source, Creator created all that is, and is all that is created. Consequently, as we human beings are too creations of Source—we too are of Source, carrying within our physical bodies Source energy to create. We are all capable and all powerful of attracting all that which we are wanting because of our of-Source energy.

Applying the Law of Attraction, we are capable of creation and manifestation through the thoughts and emotions we carry each moment of our lives. As we have thought and felt either negatively or positively toward any one particular thing in our life experiences, we have been unknowingly attracting that very thing into what we understand to be our reality. As with other universal laws, the Law of Attraction is always and forever in motion. We cannot bring ourselves to a place of pausing that which we are attracting and calling forth into our physical experience.

How we determine whether we are attracting something we are wanting into our lives over something we are not wanting is by monitoring the way we are feeling. Our feelings are our embedded indicators that display whether or not we are on the path of allowing and attracting what it is we are truly wanting.

Source is not a biased provider and will surely give to us all that we are asking for whether we are aware of it or not. It is clear now that Source is the center point through which all things come into our physical experience. We, as branches of Source energy, came forth into the physical to experience all that is and to enjoy and relish in the power we have to create. As I have expressed and shared my beliefs with individuals around the world, it is clear to me that many people hold similar beliefs or inclinations within themselves, though do not fully comprehend to which extent it can be applied into every moment of our lives. I so eagerly write to all in anticipation to fulfill my purpose in extending the truth of power we all hold within to create our own realities through the thoughts and feelings we hold.

CHAPTER 5

ASK AND IT MUST BE GIVEN

There is a common understanding circulated in and around countless belief groups and religions in which Source delivers and provides unto us all that we are asking for, and all that we are needing. I have found that many sacred books connected to these belief groups present this bit of knowledge briefly, but do not accredit this gift of creation to the degree it deserves to be recognized. In these sacred books, scattered passages are found expressing the truth that when we ask for and feel the having of what we are asking for in our vibrational being, Source brings forth into the physical. It is also written in these sacred books that Source is all knowing of what we are needing and wanting, and provides a fair compromise between need and want unto us one-hundred percent of the time. As expressed in the previous section, we as human beings—brought forth of Source, holding within Source energy—must practice awareness of our emotions triggered in experiencing the wants and do not wants, and how these emotions are vital in the very creation of our own personal realities.

I have now come to understand that the line we so successfully draw between what it is we are wanting and what it is we are needing only introduces a sense of limitedness of resources and of deservingness regarding how our life experience unfolds. We often compete with and compare ourselves to others in our world today. We have been lead to believe that how we are perceived by others is of great importance, and what we have in our physical distinguishes us as individuals. Looking further, the truth of the matter is that our individual selves are all that should be of importance and focused on as we sift and sort through the wants and do not wants in setting the foundation for the allowance of the manifestations we are calling into being.

We live in an unlimited, abundant universe of resources and experiences that are readily available for our utilization at the very moment we finally allow them into our physical experience. Often times this idea of limitedness is created and taught by those with power as they feel they are doing themselves a favor in reserving "the good stuff", or the abundance, for their use. The truth expressed is that there is no end. There is no limit in which we must forfeit or even jeopardize our wholehearted happiness and bliss. We are all entitled to and all deserving of experiencing all that brings joy into our lives through love and light. As vibrational beings, we are prewired to want and desire. Through desiring, we are internally inclined to manifest what it is we are desiring, and through manifestation, we are expanding our universe through creation.

We are naturally asking throughout our entire life experience in just the bringing ourselves towards awareness of the contrast of things that we come into contact with that bring forth either good or bad feelings. When we encounter the particular somethings in our day-to-day experience that provoke feelings of true desire and want, we must trust that we will feel happier in the having of it and in the creating of it. In believing that we will be happier in the having of what we are wanting, we are really asking for clarity, for wholesomeness, and for utter satisfaction. It is also of utmost importance that we understand that the Ask and Receive process is far from how it is made out to be in our sacred books.

By Law of Attraction, the asking and the receiving is what we as branches of Source energy have come into our physical bodies to do, and to celebrate in the mere joy of creating. In a world with billions of people, all of whom are asking, Source has readily available the equivalent of what we are asking for tenfold.

In a world where every man, woman and child trusted that Source was ready and willing to give unto them what they were asking for, there would not be any competition for success, any skirmishing of resources, or any doubt. In a world such as this, there would only be asking and receiving.

CHAPTER 6

VIBRATIONAL ESCROW

There is a naturally occurring vibrational collective unit that I like to call our Vibrational Escrow. In our Vibrational Escrow, our amounted wants and desires are continuously collecting—a sort of storage unit in which we place our wants and desires. When we see and experience all that we are wanting, we are subconsciously placing the vibrational existence of these things into our Vibrational Escrow. Alternatively, in seeing and experiencing all that we are not wanting throughout our experience, we are still placing exactly what it is we are wanting into our Vibrational Escrow through the awareness of contrast. In seeing what we do not want, we are triggering rushes of desire for that which we do want.

The very reason we call into our experience all that we shout "no" at, and all that brings us into a negative-feeling state is so that we perceive the contrast of what it is we are wanting to manifest and bring into fruition. We cannot have positivity without negativity. As we sit in our state of helplessness over an amounted debt or in frustration with a deteriorating car, we must realize that these conditions and circumstances only serve as guiding points to redirect our focus onto the contrast brought forth through these negative conditions and circumstances.

All things in our Vibrational Escrow are very much in existence. All things exist vibrationally before we physically bring ourselves to the having of them. We often get so caught up in the wanting proof and validation of seeing progress that we discredit the art of creation that is taking part just beneath the surface.

The amount of experiences in our Vibrational Escrow is immeasurable and infinite. At any given moment, we subconsciously deposit experiences into our Vibrational Escrow. All of the absolute fun in experiencing our wants and desires is being celebrated by us in our Vibrational Escrow, for if we are able to bring something into our thoughts, it is because it is already in existence in another realm of reality. We can bring ourselves into the physical reality from our vibrational reality with ease, and at any given moment.

CHAPTER 7

ALLOWING ABUNDANCE

We live in a world of infinite resources that can provide us with the energy, sustainment, and nourishment that we require to keep us alive and breathing—an abundance of resources and ideas that inspire new, and sometimes improved, methods of living. To think that there is a shortage of any particular resource-provided experience is selling ourselves short of feeling happiness and bliss in all things related. We are meant to fulfill our innermost desires and expand our universe through the creation of. As we begin to allow ourselves to come to the understanding that as branches of Source energy we have come into the physical form to create, it is only logical to then allow ourselves to bring into fruition all that we are wanting in understanding and trusting that what we are wholeheartedly wanting is of love and will impact not only ourselves positively, but all others we may cross paths with in our experience.

As we go about our day discerning the wants from the do not wants, our Vibrational Escrow is amounting in all desired experiences. Often times, we are lead to believe that working hard with the occasional lucky day is the only way to achieve success in any form of endeavor we are presented with. Additionally, we often misdirect our pride for our achievements and successes towards working hard and being diligent. I firmly express that working hard does not always have to be a requirement in allowing the widespread abundance that we so yearn to relish in. The process of leading the life we are all wanting—the happiness, the wealth, the health, and all else—is so very simple, and so very natural to us. The matter at hand is much greater than wishful thinking. The house, the relationship, the money, the health, the circumstances and rendezvous are all sure. It's sure.

The most crucial bit of attained knowledge that I am basing this entire book on is the absolute importance of a shift of perspective introduced to the way we live. In order to most easily manifest anything on any scale, we must accomplish an internal shift from a view of making things happen to one of allowing them to happen and come into our physical experiences. When we work at making things happen, we introduce great resistance into our vibration which ultimately contradicts the very thing that we are setting out to achieve. We can quite literally feel the resistance of working hard because that is what proves most successful in reaching our desired life destinations, and is what we hear most frequently from those before us—the large pill we have been lead to swallow in the morning before heading off to the assembly line we limit ourselves to. We have been forced to see things through restricted lenses in only experiencing our desired manifestations through the path most traveled instead of being encouraged to allow into our lives all that we are wanting in whichever pathways they might most easily unfold.

As we bring ourselves to the allowing of abundance, we can feel the ease of things. We can begin to feel the ease of getting the job or of meeting a soulmate, the ease of strengthening our relationships and of experiencing a flow of dollars. There is no such thing as hard work or of luck in the eyes of Source and within our internal corresponding energy in allowing ourselves abundance. However, we must understand that we cannot and most definitely will not achieve our desired success by merely asking and hoping to receive. As we bring ourselves to this allowing state, we are trusting that Source will inspire us to act in a way that sits best within us in setting out to achieve and receive that which we are wanting.

We often accredit our random and unpredicted amassed fortunes and successes to luck. As I do not believe in luck, promote luck, or wish luck unto others, I understand that the root of these so-called random jackpots of events we celebrate are truly brought forth when we subconsciously release our inner resistive state and allow ourselves to come into alignment with that which was in our Vibrational Escrow. Often times, we are wanting something so strongly that we unknowingly offer split energy and resistance towards our desire. This is commonly due to the scale on which our desire falls, making it seen as difficult or unreachable altogether. Other times, it is merely because we find ourselves attempting to find a way in which our desire will come into manifestation—consequently introducing feelings of doubt and uncertainty.

Striving to practice thoughts of deservingness and worthiness until they become of our subconscious is the ultimate token in bringing ourselves to a full, allowing state. A belief is a thought practiced time and time again until it becomes of the beholder. Truly thinking and feeling that we are worthy and deserving of all things, and putting into practice that all things are always working in our favor—either positively or negatively dependent upon our vibration—will then enable us to climb the vibrational scale of allowing greater and greater things into our experience. A great indicator of whether or not we are on the path of allowing that what we are wanting is by staying tuned in to the way we are feeling. It is important to highlight that feeling unhappy, doubtful, or impatient towards our desires after we have vibrationally asked for them to manifest into the physical is often times the very thing that is keeping us from seeing them come into fruition. When it comes to the manifestation of what we are wanting, we should feel as if we are already experiencing them now. In knowing and trusting that the universe only responds to the vibration that we give off in our now, we must feel our desires in our presence now; we must vibrationally bring ourselves to the feeling of the having of them so much so that we do not need to have them, for the feeling of having and experiencing them provides the same rush and bliss we would otherwise feel in the physical. It is when we have achieved this level of vibration of feeling the blissful presence of fruition, rather than that of discord and impatience, that we will finally allow all that we are wanting into our experience.

I very strongly wish to promote selfishness and materialism. As I have dissected into the core of each of these two heavily tainted and infamous words, a sense of clarity has been reached in my life. Selfishness in the raw is best defined as being focused on and of self, holding self with highest priority in all aspects of life. My perspective of selfishness can be best understood by using an analogy many of us can relate to. As we sit aboard an aircraft in anticipation of takeoff, airlines display safety videos in case of the rarity of an in-flight emergency. In these sometimes redundant but all very resourceful videos, we are instructed that should a decrease of cabin air pressure occur, we must first apply our own oxygen mask before we help others with theirs—even if the person we are wanting to help is a child. On a greater scale, I believe this to be true in our day-to-day lives. If we are not first and foremost selfish of our emotional, mental and physical health, how should we expect to contribute to our family, friends, and world as a whole? I would very much agree that putting others before ourselves is very appealing on paper, but it is almost detrimental when stepping back and viewing matters from a long-term standpoint. I promote full selfishness so that we are mentally, emotionally, and physically healthy and stable enough to contribute how we are called to for our children, spouses, parents, and friends.

We live in a material world, truly. All things in our physical reality are of-material, from the clothes on our bodies to the earth beneath us. To rule out any one particular material in the world we are so focused as a negative would very well be a double standard. We encounter individuals quite repeatedly who have the whole understanding backwards in that they are either too focused in the material manifestations of all that is without the root spiritual source of beingness, and those who focus so heavily on the spiritual but fail to recognize that through our spirituality, we call into being all things physical and material because it is the very expansion we are here to experience. We must not chastise those who choose to place focus on either the physical or spiritual aspect of life, but encourage them to incorporate both ends of the spectrum into a daily appreciation and celebrated bliss as both coexist and are products of each other.

The stigmas of selfishness and materialism we find in our society today carry with it a sense of shortage which we are beginning to now understand and practice is rather inaccurate. We must practice an understanding between selfishness and greed, and between materialism and neglect.

There is not a limit in which we must cap-off the extent of our experiences because of the adopted mentality of scarcity that the societal world has embedded within our vibration. It is true that those who choose to live an abundant lifestyle are just as deserving and are just as capable as those who choose to live a humble one, experiencing his own abundance in a way that sits well within him. As we go about establishing our lives, and to which extremity we wish to carry out our experiences, we must lead with an internal feeling rather than an external stance. Which experiences sit well within us are almost always not experiences that are matched with others—the naturally provided contrast of the world we live in. It would be unfair of us to deprive ourselves from experiencing all that we are wanting because of a misconception of living in a limited universe, and it would be equally unfair of us to provide anything but full support towards others for allowing into their experiences all that they are wanting. There is no limit, there is not a line to be drawn. We should encourage everyone in our experience to allow all that they are wanting—on all levels

and in all forms—as long as they are are asking

and allowing in love, and seeking clarity and a

betterment of self.

CHAPTER 8

VIBRATION IS KEY

Not very long ago, I had introduced my adopted life-perspective to a dear friend of mine over tea. He had heard of similar perspectives before, but expressed that he had not heard it as I had presented it to him. As anyone being introduced to alternate and sometimes foreign life concepts and ideas is expected to react, he shared some uneasiness regarding this shift of perspective. He insisted that there must be a point in which a line must be drawn concerning seeking one's own happiness and carrying out the selfishness that I teach and encourage. He then progressed with an example that expressed further his uneasiness: "In the extreme case of an ill-willed individual who would find happiness in bringing discomfort and harm to others, how should they be entitled to their own happiness and selfishness, and at what cost to their victims?" While this instance was very severe and deeply saddening to consider, I understood completely where my friend was coming from. Before I began to answer his question, I asked for him to bear with me as what I was about to say will initially begin as sounding very insincere.

In even an extreme situation such as this, both parties would have served as cooperative components in the manifestation of such horrible event as we are always cooperative. While it is understood how the ill-willed person would serve as a cooperative component, we must dissect how those who suffer from the actions of those exemplified play part in the greater manifestation of tragedy. We are vibrational beings and we receive and achieve exactly what it is we vibrate most strongly and most clearly. In situations that cause such distress and hurt, we must understand that we have unknowingly, or subconsciously, allowed it into our physical experience because of how strongly we held vibration to what it was we were not wanting. Rather than placing strong emphasis on the negative consequences that may derive from using poor judgment in approaching decisions, we should redirect emphasis on the feelings of assurance of safety, security, and overall wellbeing. Intimidation should never be a tactic used in teaching our youth or in preventing ourselves from harm or distress, for the stronger vibration will always present itself in our physical experience. Just as so, we often see movements of anti-war, anti-racism and all other anti-negative strides in building a safer and more accepting societal environment, however we frequently fail to understand that because we are holding the very anti portion in such high vibration, we are only attracting the very thing we are not wanting time and time again into our physical. As we become more aware and accepting of the power we hold with each day, we will begin to naturally bring ourselves to an environment full of the acceptance, peace and love without having to place so much emphasis on the negative presented in our world media as it truly serves us the very opposite of what we are internally setting out to do. We are all learning, and the sooner that we redirect ourselves towards the positive, good feeling vibrations, the quicker the Law of Attraction will bring those vibrations into our physical.

CHAPTER 9

OUR PRESENT IS OLD NEWS

Source does not take into consideration what we have in the physical and tangible now in determining what we will be dealt in the later. As we are in continuous motion, it must be understood that our present is very much in fact our past. Though it seems completely illogical, we find yet another opportunity to challenge our impressed upon ideas and beliefs of time.

As we have already set out to begin the practice of dismissing the ideas and restraints of time and other beliefs of the indefinite continued progresses of events, it is now clearer to us that this time-space reality we are living in is perceived by and understood only through the eyes of the beholder. Our present-day events are merely the result of our past thoughts and emotions that have finally broke the surface into the physical reality we call our present. As we challenge ourselves to believe that time is only a method of measurement we have created, we facilitate the allowing of the understanding that there is no difference between living any particular experience in our vibrational realities from that of living those experiences in our physical realities.

We understand that everything is energy and in constant vibration, always moving, and always moving forward. Though we may attract particular events and experiences that do not bring forth a state of feeling good, or even those that are utmost uncomfortable to experience, we must still understand that we are indeed moving forward, only allowing our lives to unfold forward in the a direction that does not match with where we desire to be. Our society has so enjoyed using the saying "taking one step forward only to get knocked two steps back" when faced with experiences that are not up to par physically with where we are vibrationally. But now that we understand that there is no moving backward, there is only moving forward, it is clear that this moving forward to be moved backward feeling is only brought forth through splitting our energy in our vibrational and our physical, and in directing our focus towards that which we are not wanting. It is true that shifting our energy from the "what is" to the "how I'm feeling" and the "what is on its way to me now" is probably the most difficult part of this greater Law of Attraction process in unlocking our entirely achievable, sought-after lifestyles and life experiences. Hopefully, however, knowing for certain that wherever we are in life now—the abundance or debt, the sickness or health, the support or isolation—is all old news proves true that we can start at any place, at any age, and in any circumstance towards the life we are sure and deserving to live.

Wherever we are now has only been a product of our past thoughts and emotions, and whatever we are in the process of allowing into our physical experience will only be a product of our current state of being and how we are feeling now. We are in constant motion, and constantly moving forward and towards what we are thinking and how we are feeling. Our power to determine in which direction we are headed is in our now. We do not have to wait for the next open window, nor do we have to wait for the commencement of the next New Year to shift our course of direction; we can fly from here to anywhere at any given second of our experience. How are you feeling now?

CHAPTER 10

THE LIVES WE LEAD ARE OF THE STORIES WE TELL

If I could have anyone take only one thing from this text, I would want for it to be the very understanding that the lives we lead are of the story we tell. As we bring ourselves

into a constant asking and receiving state—
of rendezvous with great people, great health,
career advances, financial prosperity and all else
that is important to us—we are building up
the momentum of abundance of all that we are
wanting. It is easy to build momentum in either
direction of want and that which we are not
wanting as it is all reliant on what we willingly
choose to give our attention and focus to, and
how we wish to feel as a result.

It is most rewarding to set out in this very shift of
redirecting our attention to better feeling things
merely to feel happier. When we overwhelm
ourselves with conditions and outcomes of what
feeling good will do for us and bring to us, we

lose focus on the very importance of why we are asking to begin with. We ask and receive to feel good, and in feeling good, we are in a constant receiving state. How we live in our vibrational lives is how we yearn to live in our physical, and so it must be. It is okay to want and desire because it is part of the grand purpose of expansion and growth in not only our own lives, but for those around us. We are all part of a greater network that is wired together and working together to achieve a greater good. All desires are sure if we allow them to be sure.

We often like to work backwards in jeopardizing our bliss and happiness in engaging in what we do not want for money and other physical, temporary byproducts. When we hold with utmost importance what it is we want to do with our lives and stay true to the happiness brought forth from engaging in our passions, the money will surely follow. There does not have to be such a thing as a "starving artist" for there are unlimited resources in which Source will provide all things to us into our physical. We understand that all things are already in our own personal Vibrational Escrow and the only task we have to do to access our desires is to feel happy and focused, and free of any feelings of discouragement.

We must also remember that we will never get it done. We think that once we allow the level and degree of abundance we are yearning for into our physical lives, we will never want or yearn for more because we will have succeeded. As we travel on the path towards our widespread successes and allowances, we challenge ourselves to fine-tune our own personal perspectives which then spark new desires within us. We will never get it done; we are ever-expanding beings with the limitless power to create.

I encourage you to go out and experience, to see what feels good to you through the great experiences and through the contrasts of what does not vibrationally match within. I encourage you to dare to dream and allow all things into your life experience, for all things are possible and are now knowingly accessible for your personal expansion and betterment of self. I encourage you to cherish your manifestations when allowed into your physical, and to feel good in the knowing that you are the creator of your own experience and responsible for all things in your physical experience. I encourage you to light the world in your awareness of creation. I encourage you to ask and receive, and once you've received, to ask again and continue to expand. Now is where your power lies and now is when you can start. Now, you can have and do and be anything. What will do you? How will you use your power of awareness to be a part of this vibrational shift?

Now, we know we are creators and we cherish that Source will forever support and provide. Now, we may see the love and light in others in a way we have not yet before. We will never be finished. Now what?

Printed in the United States
By Bookmasters